The urgency of now

**Duncan Green
and Isobel Allen**

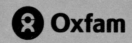
Oxfam

First published by Oxfam GB in 2008

© Oxfam GB 2008

ISBN 978-0-85598-629-2

Illustrations © John French

Book design by Kelvin Jenkins

All *Voices of the Poor* World Bank (2000) quotes can be found at:
http://go.worldbank.org/H1N8746X10

Available from:
BEBC Distribution, PO Box 1496, Parkstone, Dorset, BH12 3YD, UK
tel: +44 (0)1202 712933; fax: +44 (0)1202 712930; email: oxfam@bebc.co.uk

For details of local agents and representatives in other countries,
consult our website: www.oxfam.org.uk/publications
or contact Oxfam Publishing, Oxfam House, John Smith Drive, Cowley, Oxford, OX4 2JY, UK
tel +44 (0) 1865 472255; fax (0) 1865 472393; email: publish@oxfam.org.uk

Our website contains a fully searchable database of all our titles,
and facilities for secure on-line ordering.

Published by Oxfam GB, Oxfam House, John Smith Drive, Cowley, Oxford, OX4 2JY, UK

Printed by Oxuniprint, Unit 10, Oxonian Park, Kidlington, Oxfordshire OX5 1FP, UK.
Cover and inners printed on recycled paper made from 100% post-consumer waste.
Oxfam GB is a registered charity, no. 202 918, and is a member of Oxfam International.

Contents

www.fp2p.org

Housing for the wealthy of Lucknow (India) rises above the shacks that are home to the rag-picking community of Shanti Busti ('Peace Slum').
Photo: Tom Pietrasik / Oxfam

1. Inequality explored

There are moments when the world changes, and this should be one of them. This book sets out a vision of women and men in communities everywhere who are equipped with education, enjoying good health, with rights, dignity, and voice – in charge of their own destinies. It challenges us all to act now, together, to bring about real and lasting change.

'Inequality' is the status quo. There is huge inequality between people in their access to resources, to decision-making fora, to securing human rights and safety, and in their freedom from discrimination. Reducing inequality is both morally right and pragmatically necessary for global economic and climate security in the future. As the world enters a new era of scarcity, growing inequality could compound food, water, land, and carbon shortages, turning them into a source of conflict that destabilises whole nations. Those who feel their short-term self-interest outweighs any moral imperative to act need to be convinced. This book may help.

It asks some crunch questions. Why have countries like South Korea or Viet Nam developed so quickly, while others get stuck in poverty? Is democracy necessary for development? Why is inequality rising across the world and how have states and citizens tried to reduce it? Is tackling climate change at odds with economic growth? Is aid part of the solution or part of the problem? And what can we, as concerned citizens, do to bring about change?

It doesn't presume to have all the answers. This is a small book and these are big issues. *From Poverty to Power* is a larger book that goes into real depth; the analysis

here is based on it. If you want more, get your teeth into *From Poverty to Power*, www.fp2p.org

Meet Mai and Aminatta, two baby girls, born in Norway and Sierra Leone respectively. Mai was born in a well-equipped hospital. She and her mother survived the experience, and Mai will go to school when she is six and most probably to university. Aminatta stood a one in four chance of dying at birth; her mother a one in 47 chance of dying in childbirth. She was born at home, with no midwife, in a shanty town with poor sanitation and water supplies. If Aminatta survives, there's a one in three chance she'll never go to school. In Sierra Leone only one in four women can read and write, so university is an impossible dream. Aminatta will find it hard to get a job in a country with 80 per cent unemployment. Mai faces better prospects: if she falls ill or loses her job, there are social security systems to make sure she has enough money to survive. Aminatta has no such safety net. She will do everything earlier than Mai – start work, have children, and die. On average, women in Sierra Leone die aged 42, 40 years before those in Norway.

> **On average, women in Sierra Leone die aged 42, 40 years before those in Norway.**

From cradle to grave, these women's life chances are dominated by the extraordinary levels of inequality that characterise the modern world. Let's look at some numbers.

The total income of the world's 500 richest billionaires is higher than that of its 416 million poorest people.

Each year, the global economy churns out some $9,500* worth of goods and services per man, woman, and child – 25 times the $365 per year that defines the 'extreme poverty' of a billion human beings. Every minute of every day, somewhere in the developing world, 20 children are killed by avoidable diseases like diarrhoea or malaria, and a woman dies needlessly in childbirth. Of the three billion people living in cities today, one billion live in slums, marginalised from society and vulnerable to disease and violence. More than 880 million people are undernourished; 33.2 million are infected with HIV – 22.5 million of them in sub-Saharan Africa. The World Health Organization states that climate change claimed more than 150,000 lives per year in the last 30 years, most of them in poor countries. And according to the United Nations, it would take $300 billion a year to lift everyone on the planet above the extreme poverty line of $1 a day: that is a third of global military spending.

> **Every minute of every day, 20 children are killed by avoidable diseases like diarrhoea or malaria, and a woman dies needlessly in childbirth.**

This is a stark picture of a fractured world of rising inequality. But these easily-countable health- and wealth-related impacts are only part of the story. Inequality is about much more than differences in income. Those on the losing end experience a deep sense of powerlessness, frustration, vulnerability, and exclusion from decision-making processes, as well as a lack of access to basic public services such as health, education, and banking, even where they do exist.

* This book uses the US dollar ($) because it is the currency that is most used and recognised in global development discussions.

How long is your lifeline?
Causes of premature death worldwide*

Some causes of death receive far more human attention
– and financial commitment to their prevention – than
others. This exacerbates deep inequality.

Tobacco
4.9 million

Child undernutrition
3.5 million

**Excess weight
& obesity** 2.6 million

Air pollution (urban & indoor)
2.6 million

HIV and AIDS
2.1 million

Alcohol
1.8 million

**Water-borne
diseases** 1.8 million

**Road traffic
accidents** 1.2 million

Suicide
870,000

**Interpersonal
violence** 572,000

**Childbirth or pregnancy-
related disease** 530,000

Small firearms
(conflict and non-conflict)
248,000–367,000

Armed conflict
172,000

Terrorism
20,500

*Figures circa 2002, full table and
sources in *From Poverty to Power*
www.fp2p.org

The various dimensions of poverty and inequality reinforce each other. Many poor people suffer discrimination; but many people are poor precisely *because* they suffer discrimination and denial of their rights. In many societies, it's not income or wealth that's the causal factor, it's often gender: even relatively wealthy women face discrimination and exclusion.

In India and China, discrimination against women and girls can start before birth through selective abortion, and then continues with the relative neglect of daughters. An incredible 80 million women are 'missing' in these two countries alone, compared with the expected male/female population ratio. Black Brazilians are twice as likely as white Brazilians to die a violent death, and a third as likely to go to university. Inequality isn't restricted to the developing world. Indigenous Canadians' infant mortality rate is two to three times the national rate, and indigenous Canadians will die 20 years before the national average. Inequality can cancel out the effects of living in a better-off society: while average income is three times higher in Brazil than Viet Nam, the poorest 10 per cent of Brazilians earn less than the poorest 10 per cent of Vietnamese.

> **'Poverty is pain; it feels like a disease. It attacks a person not only materially but also morally. It eats away one's dignity and drives one into total despair.'**
>
> A poor woman in Moldova, *Voices of the Poor**

And climate change's effects will be felt more powerfully by people in the poorest countries, which have contributed least to the crisis facing the planet.

* From *Voices of the Poor*, a World Bank report (published in 2000) which surveyed 64,000 people living in poverty.

What's wrong with inequality?

Increasingly, economists recognise that inequality is damaging society by holding back economic growth.

Inequality wastes talent. If women are excluded from good jobs, half the nation's talent is squandered. If all states in India were to perform as well as the best in eradicating discrimination against women in the workplace, total output would increase by a third. When banks refuse to lend to poor people, good economic opportunities are wasted.

Inequality undermines society and its institutions. In an unequal society, elites find it easier to control governments and other institutions, and use them to further their own narrow interests, rather than the overall economic good.

Inequality undermines social cohesion. Inequality between individuals causes rises in crime, while inequality between different ethnic groups, for example, increases the likelihood of conflicts that can set countries back decades.

Inequality limits the effectiveness of economic growth in reducing poverty. A one percentage point increase in economic growth will benefit poor people more in an equal society than in an unequal one.

Inequality transmits poverty from one generation to the next. Most cruelly, the poverty of a mother can blight the entire life of her child.

The rest of this book will examine four facets of life that contribute to growing inequality, and need reform: the role of power and politics (Chapter 2), economics and markets (Chapter 3), risks and shocks such as illness or disasters (Chapter 4), and international systems and institutions (Chapter 5). Chapter 6 will focus on the role you can play. Each chapter will consider what reduces inequality and enhances development. There's no simple blueprint that works in all cases. There are though, some factors that seem to be common to the success stories; some situations that lead to more equality and less poverty than others. Chief among these factors are 'active citizens' and 'effective states'. Where they're present, inequality and poverty can be reduced.

> **'What determines poverty or well-being? The indigenous people's destiny is to be poor.'**
>
> A poor woman in Ecuador, *Voices of the Poor*

'Active citizens' are women and men who are able to exercise their rights and obligations in relation to each other, and in relation to the state. Active citizenship has clear intrinsic benefits: people having a voice and choice in determining their own destinies. But in addition, when women and men are empowered, conscious of their rights and able to demand them, they can hold states accountable, ensure inequality is reduced, and win the right to freedom and dignity.

'Effective states' guarantee security for their citizens, design and implement strategies for sustainable economic growth, are accountable to citizens and protect their rights. History shows that no country has prospered without a government that actively managed the development process.

EXHIBIT "A"
Attached to
Exhibit C
2/22/1956
WNd.

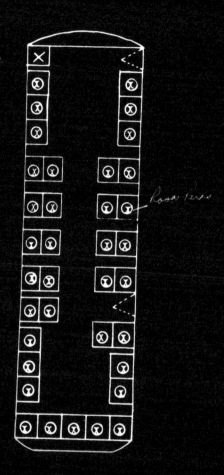

Rosa Parks

Seat layout on the bus where Rosa Parks, an African American woman, sparked the US civil rights movement when she refused to give up her seat for a white man on 1 December 1955 in Montgomery, Alabama. The diagram was exhibit A at her trial. 'When that white driver stepped back toward us, when he waved his hand and ordered us up and out of our seats, I felt a determination cover my body like a quilt on a winter night.'

National Archives and Records Administration, South-east Region (Atlanta, USA)

Effective states have governments that are willing and able to channel resources to improve the well-being of their citizens.

This book argues that working to reduce inequality involves supporting the development of active citizens and effective states. Global policies, rules, and institutions need reform so that climate change, capital flows, migration, conflict, and trade and investment rules put the interests of poor people and communities first. Active citizens around the world can support and promote the efforts of active citizens living in developing countries. Large global corporations and institutions, including charitable organisations such as Oxfam, also have a role to play. A key challenge for campaigners in rich countries is to understand that developing countries and their citizens are the real change-makers, and to explore the many ways in which we can support them.

Anything is possible. Massive shifts in the global status quo do happen, with profound and lasting effects. If the anti-slavery movement had failed, imagine the world we'd be living in now. Overcoming wasteful, destabilising inequality is the next great challenge for humankind.

'Massive poverty and obscene inequality are such terrible scourges of our times – times in which the world boasts breathtaking advances in science, technology, industry, and wealth accumulation – that they have to rank alongside slavery and apartheid as social evils.' Nelson Mandela, London, 2005

Freshta, from Afghanistan, speaks about her involvement in the 'We Can' campaign at a conference in Sri Lanka. 'We Can' aims to end all violence against women.
Photo: Annie Bungeroth/Oxfam

A visitor to Moscow's annual Millionaire Fair with a Swarovski crystal-encrusted Mercedes Benz car. The Fair caters for the tastes of the super-rich, selling private jets, yachts, and many other luxury items. Photo: Andy Hall

What's wrong with billionaires?

A common objection to trying to reduce inequality is: 'Don't be naïve. There'll always be some people who are richer than others.' But the problem is not that people are richer or poorer than each other, but the scale of that disparity. Isn't there something wrong about the systems and values that sustain a world where the combined annual income of the poorest 416 million women and men is less than that of the world's 500 richest billionaires? Let's ask a really naïve-sounding question: 'If billionaires had less, would people living in poverty have more?'

Take one example. In 2008, the world's richest man (US investor Warren Buffett) was worth $62 billion. Distributing this amount of money among the world's poorest billion people would give each person $62. That's at least 17 per cent of their annual income ($365 per year or less) and could make the difference between living in poverty and living with greater choice and opportunity.

What are the effects of this gross inequality on society as a whole? Most people aspire to wealth: they want what they see others have got. Luxuries symbolise the good life. In Colombia's jails, young men kill for a pair of Nike trainers. What does this say about how inequality affects social cohesion, the way people get along with each other? Security firms guarding the properties of the better-off with razor wire and armed guards are among the most lucrative businesses in South Africa. Inequality costs money and fuels crime: the amount people spend on protecting their luxuries could in itself provide the basics for many millions of people. The economic cost of policing, for example, is immense, let alone the costs of unfulfilled economic potential due to ill-health or lack of education.

> **Security firms guarding the properties of the better-off with razor wire and armed guards are among the most lucrative businesses in South Africa.**

Global rules seem geared towards wealth creation for the few. Laws allow businesses to have off-shore accounts and investments and thus reduce their tax bills, starving states of the money they need for roads, schools, and

**Number of billionaires in 2008
(up from 946 in 2007)**

**Number of billionaires
under the age of 40**

**The fortune of
Warren Buffett, the world's
richest man**

**The fortune of Aliko
Dangote, Nigeria's first
billionaire**

Source: Forbes.com/billionaires (Oxfam diagram)

hospitals. Could these rules be different? What alternatives are there to 'trickle down' poverty reduction, whereby the poorest people are expected to be content with the crumbs from the development table?

Billionaires symbolise the extremes of inequality, and their numbers are growing (from 946 in 2007 to 1,125 in 2008). They're at the top of a tier of rich people who claim a massive share of the world's resources – while millions of others go without. There's enough to go round. If some of the political will, ingenuity, money, and effort that supports wealth creation for the rich was transferred to supporting poor people and developing countries, inequality could be transformed.

Charities used to say that if you give a man
a fish you feed him for a day; teach him
how to fish, you feed him for a lifetime.

But…

'A *man* is just as likely to be a *woman*
and that woman aleady knows how to fish.

She would like her river left alone by illegal
logging companies or fish poachers.

She would prefer that her government
not build huge dams… dams that have
damaged her livelihoods.

She would prefer that the police not
violently evict communities to make
way for the dam.

She doesn't want charity. She would
like respect for her basic rights.'

A female village leader, Cambodia

Mrs Svey Sap Sak, Cambodia   Photo Jack Picone/Oxfam

2.
Redistributing power

Politics lies at the root of development and reducing inequality. Some people say they don't 'do' politics. That's like saying you don't 'do' breathing. Politics is simply the name for the processes through which groups of people make decisions, whether at international, national, community, or family level. Unless you live like a hermit on an ownerless, ungoverned piece of land, entirely self-sufficient, then politics affects you – and you help create it. Politics shapes the relationship between citizens and states, and is central to reducing inequality.

Politics or group decision-making is fundamentally about power: the ability to achieve a desired end with or without the consent of others. Who has it, how they wield it, why they use it – power shapes our interactions and permeates the innermost thoughts of individuals and groups.

Power relations are complex:

Power over: the power of the strong over the weak. This power can be hidden — e.g. what elites manage to keep off the table of political debate;

Power to: the capability to decide actions and carry them out;

Power with: collective power, through organisation, solidarity, and joint action;

Power within: personal self-confidence, often linked to culture, religion, or other aspects of identity, which influences the thoughts and actions that appear legitimate or acceptable.

Powerlessness is cited by poor women and men as a defining feature of their lives. They experience inequality as lack of 'voice' and lack of choice. Powerlessness can be experienced by people who are so focused on survival that they cannot plan beyond the next few meals. Or by a beaten wife in a society that condones violence against women. Or by poor farmers, whose voices carry less weight than the commercial interests of large companies. Or by people who cannot afford to send a child to school. In rich societies there are also deep inequalities of power. And that lack of power is not an accident. Unequal power relations have been created, sustained, and reinforced through long-standing cultural, religious, or state values and attitudes. Such values and attitudes have to change, along with the laws and regulations that enshrine them.

The Universal Declaration of Human Rights provides a framework that acknowledges human rights as a global responsibility. It sets out rights that states must guarantee (such as freedom from torture), rights they must respect (such as self-determination: 'people should be free to decide their own political views and pursue their own economic and cultural development'), and those they must actively promote and finance (including essential services, such as education). Protecting and respecting people's rights should be one of the core functions of government and leaders; it should be at the heart of politics. Effective governments will uphold citizens' rights to basic services such as decent health care and education, to have a say in issues that affect them, and to freedom from persecution and discrimination.

Poor women and men experience inequality as lack of 'voice' and lack of choice.

Citizens can also demand their rights. But lack of access to education or information about your rights can in itself be a symptom of powerlessness. If you don't know your rights, how can you claim them? If you are living in poverty with no access to basic health care or education, or living on the margins of society with no voice, where are you to find the energy and ability to demand your basic rights? Being able to get access to essential services and to voice your opinions can be both preconditions for active citizenship and standing up for your rights, and consequences of doing so. Collective organisation and a receptive government seem to play a large part. Consider this example of how change can happen.

In July 2007, the Chiquitano people of Bolivia won legal title to the indigenous territory of Monteverde, home to 120,000 people. The Chiquitanos had lost their land during colonisation and lost their freedom during a rubber boom in the early twentieth century. They were bought and sold along with the rubber estates where they worked. The Chiquitanos mobilised, working together with the support of an umbrella group for all eastern Bolivia's indigenous peoples, and began to assert their collective right to territory. In 1990, they organised a march to the capital. Incorporating the momentum created by such indigenous movements, Bolivia's constitution was changed to redefine the state as 'multi-cultural'. This paved the way for new laws that allowed indigenous peoples to participate in local government. In 2000, there was a more general protest at the privatisation of water services. This crisis created the context for people to demand a general 're-founding of the Republic'. Bolivia's president was thrown out of office in 2003 and people who were not part of traditional political parties were allowed to stand in local elections. In 2005, this led to big gains for indigenous women and men. 'We got a mayor elected', said a Chiquitano leader. 'Now the [regional leader] must listen to our demands.' In December 2005, Bolivia elected its first indigenous president, and people who had never before thought they could take high-level public posts became ministers.

In Bolivia, powerless people worked together to reclaim their rights. Motivated by hardship, people mobilised, supported each other through their collective organisation, and took advantage of events they had previously thought were beyond their control. The foundations of Bolivian society changed: a fundamental reworking of Bolivia's constitution allowed indigenous political participation. Once participation was allowed, it was a matter of continued concerted action and changing cultural awareness that enabled the Chiquitanos to achieve their goals, including winning back their lands. As academic Naila Kabeer says, 'From a state of powerlessness that manifests itself in a feeling of "I cannot", activism contains an element of collective self-confidence that results in a feeling of "we can"'.

Tinkering around the edges of policy could perhaps have provided some benefits to the Chiquitanos, but as long as inequality was enshrined within the state and characterised the relationship with some of its citizens, small changes were not enough to achieve the trans-formation that was needed. Active citizens spurred on an increasingly effective state.

> **Development needs governments and citizens to combine to support – and demand – greater equality.**

Good policies do not take root if the political environment is hostile to them. Development needs governments and citizens to combine to support – and demand – greater equality. A re-visioning of politics and power is required so that upholding rights, and equality, are central. Leaders should not use political power to stifle and exclude, and citizens should be supported to hold such leaders to account. All those who influence development – citizens and governments, and also the international system, companies, and non-government organisations – should take this message seriously, as we'll see in Chapter 5.

For much more on politics and power, visit the *From Poverty to Power* website, www.fp2p.org

Citizens and states: how change happens

Supporting the development of active citizens and effective states is vital to reducing inequality – but their relationship is complex, and their development isn't linear. A country's access to natural resources, its political situation, international standing, historical development, and cultural and religious make-up, to name but a few, all influence the path to development – how citizens and governments interact and change. This section explores some ideas about the relationship between citizens and states.

The actions of citizens can impel, or even compel, governments to change. Active citizen movements can make governments more effective. In Guatemala, for example, the Social Spending Observatory challenges the secrecy surrounding the state

Effective states – May Day 2006, President Morales announces the nationalisation of Bolivian gas, making more public funds available for essential services. This was in response to demands from Bolivia's indigenous social movement. Photo: Renato Guimaraes/Oxfam

budgeting process and publishes analyses of government spending. Monitoring programmes in Uganda identify and publicise corruption. In some countries, the government itself funds non-government organisations that provide checks and balances to its power and decisions.

Conversely, government policies on education, rights and identity, for example, can change citizens' attitudes, beliefs, and behaviour. This may be necessary to prevent active citizens from threatening minority rights – white supremacist movements for example. There will always be tensions between citizens and states. The challenge is to make it productive tension, placing human rights and equality at its core. Governments can encourage citizens to be active, and citizens can encourage governments to be effective.

Historically, 'effective states' have been seen as those that achieved economic growth. But well-being is about much more than growth, and states often neglect important non-monetary aspects of well-being, resulting in powerlessness and exclusion. Without active citizens holding governments to account, economic growth is likely to benefit some people far more, and at the expense of others.

Increased well-being and reduced inequality make for a happy, healthy citizenry and better workers, so it is in the interests of states economically and ethically, to encourage an active citizenry. Reducing inequality requires both effective states and active citizens. Development strategies placing rights and equality at their core – whether initiated by citizens or governments – are crucial.

The Wall Street Bull, New York – a symbol of
financial optimism and prosperity   Photo: Gary Millikan 2007

3.
Sharing wealth

Income and wealth aren't the only factors that affect a person's well-being but they are an important part of the picture. Our incomes are to a large extent governed by the operation of markets, the structures through which people buy and sell goods and services. At their best, markets are mighty engines, generating wealth and transforming people's lives and expectations. At their worst, they exclude poor people, fuel inequality, and degrade the natural world. How can markets promote sustainable, equitable growth?

Economics is the main tool used to make sense of and regulate what happens in markets.

But it has tended to equate income with well-being, even though well-being is highly influenced by power relations, discrimination, and the ability to participate in society as well. Markets that are set up to maximise income at the expense of equity and human rights will not work for development in the long term.

Development strategies often ignore or undervalue important factors. Two examples:

Unpaid work, whether caring for the sick and elderly, doing housework, or bringing up children, is not counted as part of the 'real economy'. Actually, the value of household work is estimated to be between 35 and 55 per cent of economic output. This omission particularly damages women's rights. Decisions made on this flawed analysis are likely to perpetuate inequality by undervaluing women's contribution. And there's overwhelming evidence that where there's equality for women, there's a more prosperous and efficient economy.

Similarly, the use of natural resources and resulting pollution and carbon emissions should be included in economic calculations, as the facing page explains.

...GROWTH...

...STABILITY...

INCOME...

HEALTH

EDUCATION

ENVIRONMENT

RIGHTS

Counting the environment

'Full cost accounting' is a way of pricing goods and services so their true costs, including the environmental and social costs, are included. The 'full' cost of a car includes its environmental impact, the cost of its eventual disposal, as well as its initial cost to manufacture. Depletion of natural resources and damage to the environment could be included in the calculation of a country's annual gross domestic product (GDP: the value of all goods and services produced).

World Bank economists used this approach when they estimated the depletion of natural resources and pollution damage in Bolivia in 2003. They reported that while conventional economic analysis found national savings of 12 per cent of economic output, full cost accounting showed there was really a loss of nearly 4 per cent.

Photo: Ian K. Rogers

While it's hard to put a value on how far policies support human rights, for example, at the very least governments (and international donors and financial institutions) should not ignore these factors for the sake of expediency. Either economic analysis should be viewed as just one part of a much more complex jigsaw when designing strategies, or it should make an attempt to quantify these factors.

So we need a more honest, comprehensive view of economics. What else do we need to get right to allow markets to fuel equitable development? Rural economies are of great importance to poor people because the majority of the world's poor women and men live in rural areas. Rural lives are changing fast, but two and a half billion people still live in farming families, including smallholders and labourers. Farming, then, is an essential part of the market to get right.

> **'Poor people in Tanzania have described rich people as those who set the prices, while the poor are those who are forced to accept the prices set by others.'**
>
> *Voices of the Poor*

The World Bank calculates that agricultural growth reduces poverty twice as fast as growth in other areas of the economy: the experience of countries as diverse as the USA, Viet Nam, and Costa Rica bear this out. However, increased agricultural output will only support development if small farmers get a fair share of the benefits.

Bio-piracy

Bio-piracy involves the theft and patenting of traditional knowledge and natural resources by companies without compensating the country of origin. This exacerbates inequality: industrialised countries get richer at the expense of bio-diverse poor countries. There have been recent attempts to patent the use of turmeric to heal wounds (traditional in India for thousands of years), basmati rice, the neem tree (an Indian plant used to produce medicines and pesticides), and even extracts of black pepper.

In all markets, not just rural economies, private companies can either help or hinder development. They can drive growth through job creation. But they can also exploit poor women and men and harm the environment. Developing-country governments should regulate companies moving into their markets so that citizens reap the potential benefits and are also supported to assert their rights as employees.

Oxfam has found time and again that getting organised, for example forming co-operatives, can give farmers greater bargaining power with buyers, and unionising (which needs to be legalised and supported by the state) can help ensure employers respect workers' rights.

Markets can be a force for good or for ill. Economic growth and the market structures that regulate commerce are part of the solution to poverty and can help reduce inequality. It's the aims and analysis of markets that need rethinking. They should be managed by states in the interest of their citizens and sustainable economic development.

Members of the Machuara Sangathan fishing co-operative (Sania Village, Chattapur, India) pulling in a good catch. The co-operative has helped local fishers gain control over their local ponds and so their earnings, rather than working for rich landlords. Photo: Rajendra Shaw/Oxfam

Learning from the 'Asian tiger economies'

Some common factors in states that deliver economic growth

Lessons can be learned from studying the most successful developing countries in recent years: China, Taiwan, South Korea, Singapore, Malaysia, and Viet Nam. Despite patchy records on human rights, they have grown economically and reduced income poverty. These countries differ hugely in size, the type of economy, and their politics, but their paths to development have common features from which lessons about economic success can be learned.

They governed for the future: governments wanted to transform the country, rather than just achieve short-term results or skim off wealth for the elite. Civil servants were largely selected on merit rather than personal or party connections.

They promoted economic growth: governments actively intervened in the country's economy, they built infrastructure (roads, communications, etc.) and they financially supported industries they deemed to be potential 'winners'. If companies or sectors failed to perform, the state withdrew support. They minimised their dependence on volatile sources of foreign investment by promoting internal savings and investment.

They started with equality: South Korea and Taiwan began to take off by introducing radical land reforms; Malaysia took positive action in favour of the economically excluded ethnic Malay population; these states actively integrated women into their economies.

They were discriminating in their relationships with the global economy: they used trade to generate wealth, but protected

fledgling industries. Governments actively promoted national firms, and managed foreign investment to ensure that it benefited the economy as a whole.

They guaranteed health and education for all: development is synonymous with healthy and educated populations, not least because an industrial economy requires a skilled and healthy workforce. In recent decades, many developing countries (not just in East Asia) have made enormous advances in health and education.

Some of the 15,000 members of South Africa's Treatment Action Campaign (TAC) participate in a protest march in Cape Town, in April 2006. TAC fights for rights and health care for HIV- positive people. Its successes include persuading Thabo Mbeki's government to change its policy on and investment in preventing and treating HIV and AIDS. Photo: AP/PA Photos

4.
Reducing fear and anxiety

No one's life is free of risk. There's always some insecurity: whether about jobs, health, housing, relationships, or raising children. But while rich women and men and rich countries can manage many risks and avoid some altogether, poor people and poor countries often cannot. 'Shocks' hit the poorest people hardest. A family member losing a job, or the lack of rain can sometimes literally mean the difference between life and death. Poor-country governments are often unable or unwilling to provide the protection for their citizens that people in rich countries take for granted. Shocks both help make people poor and keep them poor.

'The wealthy can recover losses in one year, but the poor, who have no money, will never recover.'
Resident of Ha Tinh, Viet Nam

The combination of active citizens and effective states can reduce vulnerability by providing 'human security'.

People are more secure when communities and countries have prepared for disasters such as floods or earthquakes. Security comes from a state that has the infrastructure to cope, the availability of emergency supplies, and the capacity to respond (through support for those left homeless, and household or personal insurance to enable rebuilding). The role of the international community and non-government organisations – NGOs like Oxfam – in providing emergency aid will be discussed in Chapter 5.

Climate change is a massive challenge to human security, and its effects are already being felt around the world, particularly in developing countries. A recent European Union report found that without action now, up to a fifth of the global population – people in coastal zones threatened by rising sea levels and natural disasters – could be homeless by 2050.

Up to a fifth of the global population – people in coastal zones threatened by rising sea levels and natural disasters – could be homeless by 2050.

Homelessness can lead to migration, which on this scale is likely to cause unrest and ultimately conflict between and within countries. The amount of fresh water available could fall by 30 per cent in some regions, causing food shortages and civil unrest. Increasing shortages of basic resources – land, water, food – could destabilise much of the planet. Price rises in some staple foods are already making life harder for poor women and men in countries both rich and poor, prompting widespread food riots and threatening to push 100 million more people into poverty. Action by states and citizens, as well as the international community, to adapt and protect people from the effects of climate change is badly needed.

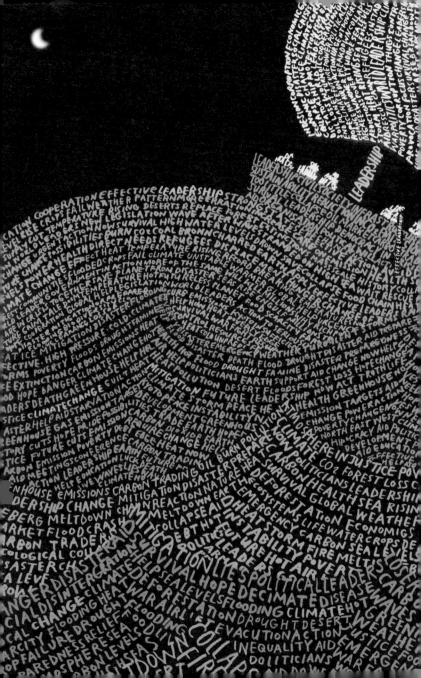

Climate change – we need to act now, but how?

Mitigation – reducing emissions to slow and stop climate change

This is the part most people know about. We must all take individual action to reduce our 'carbon footprint' and encourage our employers, health services, and schools to do the same. We must take fewer flights. We should insist that our governments set and stick to tougher targets for reducing national emissions that include strict controls on business emissions. We should lobby for internationally agreed targets. We need to do all this now.

Adaptation – building people's resilience to the impacts of climate change

Reducing people's vulnerability relies on states having national adaptation strategies, taking action to protect citizens, informing them about risks, and supporting them to make choices that will help them survive. Citizens need to be willing and able to make choices to protect themselves, whether by moving, protecting their homes, or adopting new strategies for making a living (diversifying). Being willing and able to make choices depends on having enough money and enough power to do so.

Who should pay

The implications of climate change seem clear and yet those governments and global institutions with the power to do something are dragging their feet. Part of the problem, as usual, is agreeing who should pay for it, and how much.

Financing global adaptation and mitigation is in everyone's interests – the 2006 Stern Report showed that the costs of financing adaptation and mitigation were less than the projected costs of inaction. Taking the view that the fairest way is for those most responsible for climate change and capable of affording it to pay the most, Oxfam devised the Adaptation Financing Index (AFI). The AFI uses criteria based on contributions to CO_2 emissions, population, and position in the Human Development Index (how developed the country is, including GDP and other factors) to apportion responsibility and assess capability to pay.

So which countries should provide that finance? Oxfam's AFI finds that the USA should be responsible for over 40 per cent of what's needed annually, the European Union for over 30 per cent, and Japan for over 10 per cent. Within the European Union, the top five contributors should be Germany, the UK, Italy, France, and Spain.

For more on the AFI visit:
www.oxfam.org.uk/resources/policy/climate_change
(see: 'Adapting to climate change' paper)

People wading through flood water which swept away the road to their village in Pakistan, 2007. Photo: Mirjam van den Berg/Oxfam Novib

Illness can have far-reaching effects, launching poor households into a spiral of ever-deepening poverty from which it's difficult to recover. When illness reaches epidemic levels, like HIV and AIDS, the effects are catastrophic. HIV and AIDS is spread both by personal behaviour and governments' failure to tackle it. Women aged 15–24 are six times more likely to carry the virus than men in the same age group, due to women's lack of power in sexual relationships, and the way the disease is transmitted. But it does not have to be that way. In Brazil, a combination of government investment in treatment and prevention programmes (medicines, education), and citizens changing their attitudes and behaviours, has halved AIDS-related deaths and reduced stigma and discrimination.

> **'In Burkina Faso, AIDS widows... have been chased with their children from their villages.'**
>
> *Voices of the Poor*

In rich countries, pensions, insurance, child benefit and other types of 'social protection' – ways of securing a minimum standard of living and protecting people from shocks – are the norm. Applying similar 'shock-absorbers' in developing countries can smooth the bumps. Some developing countries have already implemented such schemes. In South Africa, introducing pensions for the elderly not only helps recipients directly but also helps grandparents keep their grandchildren in school. In Brazil, families receive a payment if children attend school and are vaccinated. Social protection reduces inequality. States need to be able to raise funds (through taxation or aid)

Severo Cruz (front) with a group of Jovos volunteers. The Jovos (a Spanish acronym for young volunteers for disaster prevention) meet regularly to learn about the risks that face the Sandia River Basin in Peru, and how they can help people to cope. They have regular training courses including first aid and evacuation skills. Photo: Jane Beesley/Oxfam

to be able to afford such protection: so the more effective they are economically, the more they can afford to provide for their citizens. And the more citizens are protected, the more they are able to contribute to the economy.

One social protection idea is to guarantee all members of society a minimum income. A basic income guarantee (BIG) could be agreed nationally and set at a certain minimum level, funded by taxation or aid. More radically, there could be a global BIG, and funding could be taken from existing aid budgets or raised by, for example, new taxation on carbon use, arms, or currency transactions.

> **'And now I'm a beggar. I don't have anything... This feeling of my own powerlessness, of being unnecessary, of being unprotected is for me the worst of all.'**
>
> A poor woman in Ukraine, *Voices of the Poor*

For more detail and analysis of risks and vulnerability, and proposed solutions, visit www.fp2p.org

Can shocks be a force for good?

Shocks have often been catalysts of change. More enlightened attitudes to women workers in Europe in the wake of the Second World War and improved welfare systems in the USA after the economic collapse of the 1930s are examples of opportunities for social and economic improvements that arose from calamitous events. Shocks can also lead to negative change, like the rise of Hitler after Germany's 1929–33 economic crisis.

But most shocks merely lead to suffering. The tsunami in Asia in 2004 claimed 230,000 lives, made two million

For a healthy, happy job

Join the
WOMEN'S LAND ARMY

APPLY TO NEAREST W.L.A. COUNTY OFFICE OR TO W.L.A. HEADQUARTERS 6 CHESHAM PLACE LONDON S.W.1

A Second World War British Government poster encouraging young women to join the Land Army. The Land Army was essential in maintaining the country's agriculture and farming during and after the war.
Photo: Museum of English Rural Life, University of Reading, England

people homeless, and deprived millions more of their livelihoods. The challenge for development is to take the opportunities that come with the change that follows a shock, while continuing to support people through the crisis with the basics (water, food, and shelter) and helping them rebuild their lives. Aid donors and recipient governments should look for opportunities to make life more equitable in the longer term as well as responding to immediate crises. In Sri Lanka after the tsunami, for example, Oxfam has found that a focus on improving women's rights through aid programmes means women are now more able to make a living for themselves and have more economic and decision-making power.

So, shocks can be catalysts of positive change: a force for good in the wake of disaster.

Fight Climate Poverty campaigners at the United Nations Climate Change Conference in Bali, December 2007. Photo: Swan Ti Ng / Oxfam International

5.
Changing the rules

Power to improve life on this planet lies primarily in the hands of citizens and national governments. But the web of international institutions, laws, regulations, and agreements, collectively known as 'global governance', deeply influence the activities of both states and citizens, either supporting or restricting their power to act. Their operations can either exacerbate inequality or be part of the solution.

Good 'global governance' could help the fight against poverty and inequality in seven main ways by:

> regulating the global economy through, for example, changing the rules on trade, investment, and international financial markets;

> redistributing wealth, technology, and knowledge through aid and/or other mechanisms;

> averting climate change and health threats, through international agreements or institutions;

> avoiding war and limiting abuses during war by providing a forum for negotiation, and upholding international humanitarian laws, such as the Geneva Conventions;

> preventing powerful countries or corporations from harming weaker and poorer ones. This includes regulating the arms trade, carbon emissions, corruption, and destructive trade policies;

> providing a safety net for the most vulnerable when disaster strikes and states are unable or unwilling to cope, as through the relief work of United Nations agencies or the international community's embrace of the 'responsibility to protect';

> challenging attitudes and beliefs, for example through the Convention on the Elimination of Discrimination Against Women (CEDAW) or the Convention on the Rights of the Child.

But this massive potential is far from being realised.

Two key players are the World Bank and International Monetary Fund (collectively known, along with the lesser known regional development banks, as the International Financial Institutions or IFIs). The Bank and Fund were designed to fund programmes to address long-term development issues and lend money in financial crises, respectively. Basing many of their policies on the flawed economic model discussed in Chapter 3, some of their strategies of the last 30 years have caused considerable harm. In 1999, they announced that poverty reduction would be placed at the heart of policy design, but in practice some aspects remain unchanged or are changing far too slowly. They continue to pressurise developing countries to open their markets to international companies, deregulate financial sectors, and cut state support for farming and industry.

Good 'global governance' could help the fight against poverty and inequality, but this potential is far from being realised.

The IFIs could change in several ways. In order to support development led by states and citizens, the IMF could rein in its hands-on involvement in developing countries, except when approached for a loan or to provide advice. The World Bank and the IMF could give more power to developing countries to design their own development strategies by removing the link between IFIs' policy advice and lending. They could also change their governing structures, which are dominated by developed countries: sub-Saharan African countries comprise 27 per cent of member countries but have only 8 per cent of the votes in the lending arm of the World Bank. They should also end the outdated practice of the

USA always choosing the head of the World Bank, while Europe selects the boss of the IMF. The IMF needs to radically rethink its analysis of what matters in development, while the World Bank must work out how to bridge the gap between what it says and thinks in Washington, and what it actually does in developing countries. They could also increase their support for 'global public goods' such as technological advances in health or agriculture.

International trading systems urgently need reform. Rich countries use inflated tariffs (taxes on imports) to keep out developing-country exports. Rich-country support to agriculture, through farm subsidies and other measures, amounts to $280 billion a year, more than double the value of global aid. This allows some producers in the USA and European Union to export at less than half the cost of production, undercutting developing-country producers. Rules also force poor countries to reduce their own tariffs on imports, cutting off a source of government revenue.

> **Developed countries used tariffs and other measures to protect their fledgling industries when they were developing, but don't allow today's developing countries to do the same.**

The rules (including those set by the World Trade Organization) protect developed-country interests, prevent developing countries from competing, and allow rich-country exporters to swamp developing-country markets. Developed countries used tariffs and other measures to protect their fledgling industries when they were developing, but international trade rules don't allow today's developing countries to do the same.

While rich countries focus on helping money, goods, and services flow freely around the globe, less energy is devoted to managing flows of people. Yet migration could help millions of families escape from poverty. Every year, migrant workers send home money equal to over twice the value of global aid. The money is typically spent on basic family needs, including education and health care. Migrants need support from both their home and their receiving countries to ensure their rights are respected and to provide legal protection. An international system to increase the flows of temporary migrants could ease fears in recipient countries, reduce discrimination against migrants, and ensure migration contributes even more to development.

Transnational corporations (TNCs) are global players, and can be a force for good or ill. They can bring employment and wealth to communities or exploit workers, the environment, and natural resources. National governments should regulate businesses, but on a global level, TNCs should accept some responsibility for all whose lives they affect, not only their direct employees. It's starting to happen: major clothing brands are accepting responsibility for working conditions in their suppliers' factories (a result of sustained consumer activism), but action is needed across the board. Firms should be more transparent about their environmental and social policies and impacts, so that active citizens and governments can hold them accountable for their actions. TNCs should be held legally responsible for any environmental or social harm that results from their activities.

When TNCs pay their taxes, the revenue can pay for more schools and hospitals and help transform the economy. But large corporations have numerous strategies for avoiding taxes. Overall, the developing world is missing out on an estimated $385 billion a year (five times the volume of global aid) due to tax evasion and avoidance.

As we've seen, global action to prevent catastrophic climate change is now urgent. Climate change will have impacts that cross all borders: shrinking resources, rising food prices, and increased pressure (social and financial) from migration due to loss of land. Action on a global scale can happen quickly and effectively: when the global community reacted to the SARs outbreak (Severe Acute Respiratory syndrome, a disease which killed almost 800 people in 2002–03), it contained what could have been a global epidemic in just four months. Climate change must be approached with even greater urgency – though it will of course take longer to implement all that is needed.

The international community has seen some successes in the areas of aid and humanitarian response to natural disasters and conflict. Aid is discussed below.

Internationally, institutions like the United Nations broker peace with governments through diplomatic efforts, and along with non-government organisations (like Oxfam) provide sanitation, shelter, health care, and food aid to those affected by disasters or conflicts. This safety net provides support in times of crisis. There have been important global agreements, such as the Landmines

Ban of 1999, and the decision to negotiate an Arms Trade Treaty, but global efforts are regularly held back when donors don't deliver. Political considerations can drive choices about where to offer aid, military, or diplomatic assistance (how much attention is this particular crisis getting from rich-country citizens and media?). This leads to 'forgotten' emergencies, where people continue to be at risk because their particular brand of crisis isn't in favour with the global community.

When the small east African nation of Djibouti was hit by a severe food crisis in 2005, appeals for help raised only about one third of the amount needed, or just $96 per person affected. By contrast, the huge publicity surrounding the Asian tsunami of 2004 helped raise over four times more aid than was actually requested, or $1,241 per person.

For more detail and analysis of the international system and the kinds of reforms needed to make it work better for development, visit www.fp2p.org

Does aid do harm?

Aid is cash, goods, or services transferred from rich countries to poor ones (whether through governments, international institutions, or NGOs). It sounds like a good idea but could aid actually undermine citizens and states?

There are ongoing arguments about the quantity of aid. Many countries have yet to fulfil the pledges of increases made in 2005 at the G8 meeting at Gleneagles, for example. There are also questions about the quality of aid: how it's planned and delivered, and what effects it has.

There's no point ramping up the amount of aid if it's ineffectually delivered.

Aid can work: the 'Education For All' initiative has funded an extra 20 million school places since 2000. Poor-country governments drew up plans for increasing investment in education: 30 countries have been funded and, encouraged by citizens' campaigns, 70 countries are now spending more on education.

'Good' aid is based on a realistic assessment of what's needed, which is best done by people in-country with local knowledge, and delivered through national governments and organisations. Aid effectiveness must be monitored, but not hampered by the bureaucracy that has plagued some aid programmes. Uganda, for example, dealt with 684 different aid agreements with many donor governments between 2003 and 2006.

> **Badly delivered aid can actually undermine state effectiveness.**

Badly delivered aid can actually undermine state effectiveness by encouraging governments to put donors' demands before those of citizens. Funding for national organisations to hold governments to account on spending can have an impact. Aid delivered through strengthened state structures is better than setting up organisations that work in parallel to the state.

Oxfam campaigners dress up as the G8 leaders with Pinnochio noses in the run-up to the G8 Summit in Rostock, Germany, reminding the leaders that they have promised to deliver an extra $50 billion in aid and need to keep their promises. Photo: Craig Owen/Oxfam

Aid donors cannot simply turn their backs on fragile and corrupt states. People living in these countries tend to be among the most in need of assistance, yet the infrastructure for delivering aid is often weak, with aid prone to theft. The gut reaction of politicians to deny aid to such regimes, unfortunately, often exacerbates the problem.

So what can aid donors do? Aid can be directed at basic services, increasing public sector wages and reducing the incentives for bribery or corruption. Governments can be rewarded for progress on relieving poverty, while aid simultaneously funds citizen-led organisations and the media to hold them to account.

Kenyan arms campaigner Julius Arile in New York to present Oxfam's Million Faces petition to the then UN Secretary General Kofi Annan. The United Nations voted in favour of an international Arms Trade Treaty and Julius even managed to take time out to win a 5km 'stop the violence' race. Photo: Cardina Penafiel/Oxfam

6.
Let's get urgent

This little book has set out some of the biggest challenges facing the world today. It argues that change is both possible and desirable because inequality is immoral and also because it's unsustainable, wasteful of human potential, and risks undermining the economic growth that has been lifting women and men out of poverty.

It is also no exaggeration to say that the risks posed by climate change could destabilise much of the planet in our lifetime.

The power to really change the world by tackling inequality and poverty lies primarily with developing world citizens and states. But in our integrated, connected world, everyone, wherever they live and whoever they are, has a part to play. Global citizens in a global movement for change can provide vital support to the efforts of states and citizens in poor countries, and challenge a global status quo that perpetuates inequality and poverty. We in the North are not in the driving seat of development, but we bear a great responsibility to clear the road.

The agenda for action for anyone concerned about inequality – and climate change – is first and foremost to 'stop doing harm'. This means assessing the arguments presented here, and then looking at our own attitudes and behaviour to see how far they support, or undermine, active citizens and effective states. Recycling or giving to charity are important acts of citizenship, but may not be enough. More vital still is being part of a movement of people who believe that inequality can and should be challenged: a critical mass of informed, active citizens who stand in solidarity with active citizens in developing countries and with governments that are trying to be more effective.

Sometimes 'standing in solidarity' can sound as if it's about doing nothing, but thinking the right things while you do it. It should mean living our lives according to our principles, speaking out in favour of justice, and recognising the possibility of change. Inspirational individuals and movements of people can, and have, changed the world: after all, governments and